Hard Money

How to build wealth without winning the lottery

by John West

Copyright © 2018 John West

Cover illustration © John West

$

All rights reserved. This book or any portion thereof may not be reproduced or used in any manner whatsoever without the express written permission of the author, except for the use of brief quotations.

$

DISCLAIMER

This book is for informational purposes only and is not intended as legal, tax or investment advice. It merely sets out what has worked for the author, and is intended to assist readers to make their own decisions and choices. Please consult professional advisors regarding your own particular circumstances, or at least consider the appropriateness of the information with regard to your own objectives, financial situation and needs, before acting on the information.

Chapter 1 – Last Chance

This book might not be for you.

If you would rather live a happy life, with a loving partner, a functional family and a large circle of friends, then read no further.

And that's okay. Most people would rather live that way. Maybe people SHOULD live that way.

If you want an album full of happy photographs, testament to a life lived to the full - burn this book.

Do it now, before it infects you with the insane desire to build wealth and achieve financial freedom.

Chapter 2 – On The Other Hand

Still with us?

$

"No warning can save people determined to grow suddenly rich," said Lord Overstone in the 19th century.

$

Except that this is not a get-rich-quick book. That would be "Easy Money." You can find dozens of those books online, detailing many ways to make it big. Some of these schemes work for some people some of the time. When they don't work, most people give up and remain tied to the hamster wheel till their dying day, exhausted and drowning in debt.

But there is a choice you can make. **You can choose to work hard for as many years as it takes to scrape together enough cash to break those chains and live a life free from financial worry. To stop living from paycheck to paycheck.**

$

You may then decide to carry on working, in the same industry or elsewhere. Unfortunately, most people struggle for years in jobs they hate. Try to avoid this. If you can't do well at a job you love, either do well at a job you hate, or struggle in a job you love.

If you want to learn how to focus on building wealth, the hard way, then read on.

$

Everybody wants to win the lottery. But not everyone buys a ticket.

The same principle applies here.

Everybody wants to build a nest egg, to scrape together enough money to live his or her dreams. But very few people are willing to put in the effort and make the sacrifices required to make it happen.

The hardest part is often just starting the journey. Accepting that you need to change and committing to it.

You have a very slim chance of winning the lottery. Don't let that stop you buying a ticket. Stranger things have happened. But you have a much better chance of building wealth slowly, over 20 or 30 years. If you have the right mindset.

If you want it bad enough.

$

Let me make this crystal clear before we carry on.

$

THERE IS NO MAGIC FORMULA THAT CAN INSTANTLY FIX YOUR FINANCES.

$

If that's what you were looking for - please refer to Chapter 1.

Instead, this book will remind you of the unpopular old fashioned notion that if you stay focused, work hard and save your money, it might just pay off at the end of the day.

If you would rather be a rock star or an actor, I wish you the best of luck. The world can never have too much music.

Don't try to make money writing books. Trust me. Rather go with the rock star thing.

And be sure to buy that lottery ticket on the way to your first gig. Just in case.

Chapter 3 – What's It All About?

I'm glad you asked.

This book was written to help people manage their personal finances and their attitude to, and relationship with, money. Small changes in attitude, sustained over lengthy periods, can have far-reaching effects.

With the right attitude, you can avoid financial pitfalls and slowly build wealth over the course of your working life. The right attitude, combined with focus, discipline and determination.

$

Building wealth is not the same as making money. That's like saying that having children is the same as going on a date. One can sometimes lead to the other, but it takes hard work, and the result is never guaranteed.

$

Rapper M.C. Hammer topped the charts in the 90s with U Can't Touch This, and made over $30 million. But excessive spending – including his giant mansion and the huge entourage he hired to accompany him everywhere he went - bankrupted him by 1996.

Don't be like M.C. Hammer.

$

Too many people worry too much about money while overlooking the other wonderful things in their lives. Some of my closest friends fall into this category. I keep reminding them to count their blessings.

In the opposite category are those who have made decent money over the years, by following the principles set out in this book. But they never married. Their children live on the other side of the world. And their dogs grew old and died.

Where would you rather find yourself when you hit middle age?

$

Ideally, you should find a balance between work and family. A loving partner, happy children, friends, family holidays, stimulating hobbies, two Chihuahuas and a white picket fence.

Not too many children, though. They'll eat through your money faster than those Chihuahuas. Do yourself and the world a favour. Let's keep it to 1 or 2, at the most. And wait for the right time.

Some people achieve this balance, at least some of the time. Some never do.

$

Let me stress up front that I am not a relationship counsellor. Nor am I a psychiatrist. Or even a registered financial advisor. What I am is a financial manager and money coach who believes he understands numbers and how to work with the energy called money. So I will be giving you some tips on how to build a moderate degree of wealth during your lifetime.

You may end up with a dysfunctional family. Only a few close friends. A dog that doesn't recognize you when you drag yourself home at the end of another 12-hour day. Be wary of this. Try to keep some perspective. After all, it's only money.

$$\$$$

Really.

It is.

Chapter 4 – Sacrifice

Several years ago, a young lady started work in a company I managed. She was married with a child. She lived more than an hour away from the office, so she spent a lot of time driving to and from work. But she was determined to build a solid career for herself and her family, and this was a great opportunity. She was also studying part-time towards her accounting degree. So after a long day at work, and a long drive home, she would cook dinner for her family, put the baby to bed, then hit the books.

I was exhausted just hearing about it.

She asked my advice. Whether she should put her studies on hold while she threw herself into her new job and worked her way up. We discussed the pros and cons, short-term versus long-term.

She also mentioned that she was having trouble in her marriage. Her husband was feeling neglected, and wanted her to spend more time with the family.

I told her that she needed to make some decisions. I couldn't see any way she could possibly juggle all these balls at the same time.

Then she fell pregnant with their second child.

She resigned before the end of the month.

$

Don't take on too many challenges at once. You are not superhuman. Probably not, anyway. There are special individuals who manage to accomplish many great things during their lifetimes. You may or may not be one of them.

On the assumption that you are not, decide what you want most. Write it down. Make a plan. And work on it. Every. Single. Day.

$

Heed the words of Maria Forleo, life coach and motivational speaker - "Success doesn't come from what you do occasionally, it comes from what you do consistently."

$

Work colleagues have always driven more expensive cars than me. Cars they couldn't afford. I know this because they would be in my office every few months asking for a loan.

Don't be fooled by other people's expensive accessories. Flashy cars, big houses, designer clothes, expensive jewellery. They probably can't afford them. Neither can you.

Not yet.

$

Mark Twain, one of America's greatest writers and perhaps its first modern celebrity, declared bankruptcy in 1893 at the age of 60. A bad investment in the new Paige typesetting machine, and financial problems at his publishing house, swallowed the money he had made from his writing career – along with his wife's inheritance. He managed to transfer all of his copyrights into his wife's name before he went under.

He quipped that he had learned "not to invest when you can't afford to, and not to invest when you can."

Don't be like Mark Twain. Unless it's in the field of writing.

$$

Life happens. There will be distractions. There will be new opportunities. New challenges. New priorities. You will need to make hard choices along the way. Money will not always be the most attractive option, when weighed against family, romance, adventure, fame.

Choose 1 option. Choose 2. Decide what you want and go after it, with single-minded determination. Don't let anyone or anything stand in your way. Life is short. Money may make it easier, but money really can't buy happiness.

I can't help you with the other alternatives. But if you still choose to focus on building wealth, read on.

Chapter 5 – Games People Play

"Fame? Fortune? Happiness? The Choice is Yours!"

$

In 1955, Parker Brothers brought out the first edition of a board game called Careers.

According to their rulebook - "The object of this game is to 'succeed' by earning Fame, Happiness and Money. This is done by going through the various occupations on the board such as University, Farming and Big Business. Each player decides, as in real life, what his or her own success formula will be. The first player to achieve or exceed their own success formula is the winner of the game."

$

As in real life?

Here was a board game teaching children that you need to decide up front what you want. What you can live with. What you can't live without.

Surely more practical than discovering who killed who in which room.

$

Noted sociologist and author James Cook Brown developed the game as a response to what he perceived as the 1950s focus on purely financial success. He felt that success in life should also embrace less material goals. He later redesigned the game, bringing in aspects such as Virtue, Enlightenment and Power, but these were never incorporated into the manufactured board game.

I couldn't have helped you with any of these. Although I did say you could be a rock star.

$

Einstein's definition of success was that it equaled X plus Y plus Z. X is Work, Y is Play, and Z is keeping your mouth shut.

$

In the published board game, Fame, Happiness and Money points were all roughly equivalent to one another. You earned these by entering occupations and landing on the relevant squares. You could also buy Fame or Happiness if you had enough cash, or gamble your cash in the casino.

$

In 1989, Pamela Anderson, wearing a Labatt's Beer T-shirt, was watching a football game in a Vancouver stadium when she appeared on the Jumbotron screen. The fans went wild. Labatt's jumped on the opportunity and hired her as a spokesmodel. She went on to appear on the cover of Playboy that same year. And the rest is history.

Fame = sorted.

But after a successful career and 3 unsuccessful marriages, Pam spent too much money renovating her home, and realized that she couldn't pay the back taxes she owed. She declared bankruptcy in 2012.

Don't be like Pamela Anderson. But only where money is concerned.

$

Players in the game earn salaries that increase and decrease depending on circumstances and education levels. They also draw Opportunity and Experience cards. They can end up in Hospital or Unemployed. They can retire to Paradise Island once they have completed an occupation 3 times (allowing them to pass the Payday square more rapidly and collect more salary). And they can declare Bankruptcy if they have to make a payment that they can't afford to make.

$

Donald Trump has frequently used America's laws to his advantage, putting several of his companies into bankruptcy over the years as a strategic business decision. Between 1991 and 2009, various casinos and hotels declared bankruptcy, although he himself has never been bankrupt.

Don't be like Donald Trump. Please. Just don't.

$

Can you apply these rules to real life? Of course you can.

Decide on your success formula. Set yourself a goal. Establish a timeframe. Work as hard as you can for as long as you have to.

Always keep in mind that, unlike the board game, you can reprioritize at any point. If your old success formula isn't working for you, stop. Think. Think again. Then decide what you want, set the goal, establish a timeframe, and go after it.

$

But be careful what you wish for. You might just get it.

Chapter 6 – Equations

This is not a university textbook. We won't be exploring technical mathematical models relating to stock valuations.

These are just some basic formulas that you already know. If asked, you could list them yourself. But people lose sight of them, and complicate their own lives unnecessarily.

$

Over the years, many people have asked me to help them with their finances. After looking at their budgets and bank balances, I would advise where they could cut some expenses, juggle month-end payments slightly better to cover high-interest accounts first, maybe even consolidate their debt into a mortgage and save on interest. Sometimes, they would tell me that they NEEDED their DSTV. The kids HAVE to go to that private school. Give up the MASERATI? AND the holiday home? AND skip the annual cruise around the Mediterranean?

I'd be frustrated. They'd be frustrated. Nothing would change.

$

So to kick things off, let me state clearly, at the risk of repeating myself, that **THERE IS NO MAGIC FORMULA THAT CAN INSTANTLY FIX YOUR FINANCES.**

Nowhere in this book am I going to reveal the secret investment fund where wealthy people achieve astronomical overnight growth with no risk. This fund doesn't exist. If that's what you were looking for - please refer to Chapter 1.

$

Most financial questions don't have quick and easy answers. "Where should I invest for the best returns?" "What if I want to double my money?" "Will I have enough to retire?" The answers to these questions require an understanding of the time you have left to save or invest, your investment goal, your attitude towards risk, the current state of the world economy, your monthly expenses, and various other factors that are beyond the scope of this simple book.

Nothing worthwhile is ever easy.

$

That's why this book is called Hard Money. Because it's hard work. It requires a major shift in attitude towards the energy known as "money." But if you're willing to make some sacrifices, applying these principles is probably your best chance of achieving some kind of financial independence during your lifetime. Just think carefully before deciding what you are willing to sacrifice along the way. Some decisions can't be undone.

$

<u>Income – expenses = surplus/ (shortfall)</u>

Simple enough, right? If you spend less than you earn, you will have cash left over. If you spend more than you earn, you will have a shortfall.

You may have noticed that I did **NOT** say, "if you earn more than you spend." Spending less and earning more are **NOT** the same thing. This is an important distinction, critical to your new attitude.

Now that you have taken the decision to improve your financial situation, this is the next major shift in the way you look at money. Take a moment to digest this point. Don't carry on reading until you've grasped the subtle but vital distinction between those 2 statements.

DO NOT focus on trying to earn more than you spend. Get that idea out of your head. Your goal should be to **spend less than you earn.**

$

Happy with this first equation? Makes sense, right?

Okay, now let's turn that concept upside down and adjust your attitude again.

Pay yourself first.

Save BEFORE you pay the bills.

$

Save as much as you can. Every month. Set up a debit order that runs just after you receive your salary, moving money into your savings account. You won't notice this money was there, and you won't miss it.

$

What's that you say? You can't afford to save money? Your bills drain every last penny from your bank account every month?

Who controls those bills, those annoying debit orders? No, it isn't your bank manager. Or your creditors.

Try again.

The bills are the result of previous decisions you made. Now it's time to make fresh decisions.

$

Save a budgeted amount every month before you are tempted to spend that money on new shoes. AND manually transfer anything that's left over after the ESSENTIAL bills have been paid.

This is where your attitude towards money is so important. You need to shift your focus, to see saving as an end in itself, a goal to be achieved, rather than a byproduct of your income less your expenses.

So let's adjust this equation. Let's agree that **Income – savings = expenses.**

$

While there are ways to increase your income, it's pretty much fixed at any point in time. Don't let that limit you in terms of building wealth. Decide how much you want to save. Set yourself a target for the end of the year. Make it a stretch, but not completely unreachable.

Then look at the resulting equation. Deduct the monthly savings amount from your net income. This tells you how much you have left to spend every month.

We'll discuss this in more detail in the following chapters.

$$\$$$

Think of kids being offered 1 marshmallow now or 2 marshmallows later. It's called deferred gratification. You can spend your money now, or save it, grow it, and have more to spend later.

Your patience and sacrifice will be rewarded.

Don't be like the greedy kid.

$$\$$$

<u>Savings x 12 = annual increase/ (decrease) in wealth</u>

If you spend less than you earn for 12 months, your wealth will have increased by the end of the year.

It really is that simple.

We won't be covering stock market investments in this book. My aim is to get you to the point where you are saving regularly and have scraped together enough cash to start dabbling with more sophisticated investments. These higher risk investments are more volatile and could increase or decrease your wealth no matter what you do on a monthly basis, although – over the long term – they should result in higher growth.

$$\$$$

Actor William Shatner requested stock options instead of cash when he was hired to be the face of Priceline.com in 1997. His wise negotiating paid off over the years when the company's stock went through the roof.

He is quoted as stating that if saving money is wrong, he doesn't want to be right.

Be like William Shatner.

$$\$$$

<u>Income = net salary + investment income + other income (part-time work, lottery winnings, garage sale)</u>

Most of your initial savings will come from your salary. Later on, we'll discuss some ways to protect your salary, to keep your job and to maximize the income you earn from it.

In these initial stages, some people find it helps to take on a second job, even if it's only on weekends. Especially if they need to settle a mountain of debt before they can start saving properly.

As you build your wealth, you will start to earn more and more interest, maybe some dividends. You will also experience capital growth when you diversify into other investment types. These all add to your "income."

Your ultimate goal might be to reach the point where your passive income and capital growth from investments is enough to cover your monthly expenses. At that point, you can tell your boss what to do with his 9 to 5.

$

<u>Assets − liabilities = net wealth</u>

This is your personal balance sheet. We'll explore it a bit more in later chapters.

List and total all your assets – your bank accounts, your house (market value), your car, your jewellery – and deduct all your debt – overdraft, mortgage, balance owing on your car, credit cards, loans, store accounts. The result is how much you are worth. Financially, not as a human being.

This might be a negative number, in which case you have more debt than assets. This is a problem. You are actually insolvent. This isn't necessarily the end of the world. You may be able to juggle your cashflow indefinitely, robbing Peter to pay Paul. You might even be able to pull yourself out of the situation, by settling your debts over time. If not, you may be forced to declare bankruptcy.

$

Let's distinguish between fixed assets and liquid assets. Fixed assets include your house, car and jewellery, solid things you own. Liquid assets include your bank accounts and investments, amounts that you can cash in at any time to pay bills or settle debts. Fixed term investments, which you can't touch until the due date, form a different class of asset, for present purposes.

High earners often strive to accumulate fixed assets, believing this is the way to build wealth. But they often destroy their liquidity along the way. So they end up owning lots of fixed assets, but with huge debts, large monthly instalments and no available cash.

There are two ways to become insolvent. Having more debts than assets, or not being able to meet your financial obligations as they become due. The second one tends to creep up on people, resulting in a sudden sale of assets at less than their actual value in order to generate cash and avoid bankruptcy.

$

"How did you go bankrupt?" a character asks in Ernest Hemingway's "The Sun Also Rises."

"Two ways," Mike replies. "Gradually and then suddenly."

Don't be like Mike.

$

Millions of people are happy to live this way, struggling year after year from one paycheck to the next. Either because they have overextended themselves on acquiring fixed assets, or because they have more debt than they can afford.

Don't be like these people.

$

The Rule of 72

Albert Einstein called compound interest the eighth wonder of the world. Earning interest on interest, year after year, can double your savings. Then double them again. And again.

Years it will take to double your savings = 72 / interest rate.

So if your savings are growing at 6% per annum, your money will double every 12 years. In an investment earning 10%, you'll have twice as much after 7.2 years.

$

This is a rough rule to use for quick mental calculations, to give you an idea of how your money can grow. It becomes less accurate with rates above 10%. 72 is used because it can be divided by most common numbers. Using 70 would give similar results. This is referred to as the 7-10 rule.

The important principle is that while 7% might not seem like a huge return, earning this rate will effectively double your money every 10 years.

$

Note my use of the word "every." You can double your initial savings, then double them again, and again, and maybe yet again. The trick to compounding is to start early enough. No amount of extra saving later in life can compensate for lost compounding years.

$

This book was written at the start of 2018. Global interest rates are about to start moving up again. Keep an eye open for the best rates. Look around for balanced mutual funds offering better rates at SLIGHTLY more risk.

Consider using a tax-free savings account if these are available in your country. No point giving away any more than you have to in terms of tax.

After all, in the words of Grouch Marx - "What do you think the government does with your (tax) money? Spends it on a woman? Gets drunk? Or plays the ponies? That's what you might do with the money, or if you have to get personal, what I do."

Chapter 7 – Increasing Income

Many people trying to build wealth believe the secret lies in increasing their income. Make that one big sale. Wait for the next promotion. Have a lucky night at the casino.

Nothing could be further from the truth. People generally have very little control over their income. Even salespeople are at the mercy of their customers, the economy, company downsizing, and their own health.

We've all heard about people who have won the lottery, or received an inheritance, and blown it all. This kind of financial disaster isn't limited to us normal people.

$

Actor Johnny Depp's lavish lifestyle landed him in court in 2017, when he tried to sue his former managers for blowing tens of millions of dollars. They countersued, claiming that, despite repeated warnings, Depp simply could not afford his extravagant lifestyle, which included paying more than $3 million to shoot Hunter S. Thompson's ashes from a specially made cannon. His expensive divorce didn't help, either.

Don't be like Johnny Depp.

$

Building wealth is not about making money or accumulating expensive toys. And as far as salaries go, it's not the size that matters, it's what you do with it.

$

There is **NO MAGIC FORMULA** to triple your income overnight. This can be done, hypothetically, in the worlds of hedge funds and cryptocurrencies. But these methods are never guaranteed. With the chance of great reward comes great risk. You could lose everything. If you ignore my advice and that happens, please don't tell anyone that you read this book.

$

Make your money work as hard as you do. Ensure that time is on your side, no matter how old you are. Use the magic of compounding.

Invest most of your annual bonus. Unless you still have debt to settle, in which case that might make more sense, depending on your individual circumstances. Keep some of the bonus to treat yourself, so that being financially responsible doesn't drain all pleasure from your life.

$

Many people work astonishingly hard to stay poor. They receive a bonus or an increase, and immediately plan how to blow it on a bigger house or a faster car.

They may convince themselves that they are investing in property. But owning a more expensive house than you need is seldom a sound financial investment.

Or they tell themselves that they deserve a bout of retail therapy, because they've worked so hard and done so well.

Fair enough. You may decide to do that too. Just keep in mind that this is a choice. Not necessarily a good choice or a bad choice. But it needs to be a conscious choice. Because it will have consequences.

$

Singer Michael Jackson couldn't repay the $25 million loan he took out for Neverland. So in 2007, the most successful entertainer of all time, with thirteen number one singles under his belt, declared bankruptcy.

Don't be like Michael Jackson.

$

After blowing your bonus on a bigger house or a faster car, you may find yourself standing still financially. Back where you started in terms of building wealth.

In actual fact, you are not standing still. You are now going backwards.

$

By increasing your standard of living – aka your monthly expenses - you are making it that much harder to cover them in the event of illness, unemployment, or unforeseen (but guaranteed to happen at some point) expenses.

You have effectively built yourself a bigger hamster wheel. Now you need to keep running faster and faster to keep it turning.

A bad month or two could wipe out your savings.

$

This tends to hit hardest those who think they have a lot of money. This is one of the main differences between those who build wealth gradually, and those who just have a lot of money. Builders value it more. You will have worked harder to get it, and you won't give it away easily.

It might not be sexy to tuck money away in a savings account every time you earn a bonus, or to bump up your monthly savings when you receive an increase. Not as sexy as that new Maserati you've had your eye on. But how sexy is begging your family for a handout when the Maserati has been repossessed and the bank has taken away your mansion?

If you prefer the sexy route, please refer to Chapter 1.

If you'd rather work slowly and steadily towards the time where you don't need to live from paycheck to paycheck, read on.

Chapter 8 – Work Ethic

The average person is expected to spend around 90 000 hours at work during their life. 8 hours per day, 5 days a week, assuming 2 weeks off each year for good behaviour. This ignores travelling time, which could easily consume another 20 000 hours.

The average person thinks this is the only way to live. Because their parents did it, and all their friends are doing it. Most importantly, because society expects it.

$

In return for the lives that they sell, piece by piece, month by month, they are rewarded with just enough cash to feed and clothe themselves and build a comfortable home where they can rest and regain enough strength to do it all again for another month.

The average person doesn't mind this. The job is not their top priority. They put up with it in order to spend time with their friends, families, pets, and hobbies, in between, when they are not working. All they want is the illusion of safety and security that comes with working for a salary.

$

That's life, they say. It's the way the world works.

But what if you were to throw yourself into your job, in fact turn it into a career? Work so hard, and so smart, and so well, that you could squeeze those 90 000 hours into 20 or 30 years instead of

45? What if you could work your way up, earning promotion after promotion, increase after increase, and healthy bonuses – not limited to one a year – for a job well done?

And what if you were to invest most of this money, so that after 20 or 30 years it had grown to the point where you had enough capital to generate a passive income that covered your monthly expenses?

See the next chapter for advice on how to control those expenses, otherwise you might never have enough income to cover them.

$

Don't chase money directly, for its own sake. Focus on doing your job, all day, every day, putting in the effort and the hours. The money will come, but not if it's your main focus. This sounds like a paradox. It makes no sense. It's just the way it works.

You want to make sure that you add as much value as possible, so much so that you become an integral part of the company. Nobody is indispensable, but you need to ensure that you are at least difficult to replace. That they would notice your absence.

If a temp could do your job, you need to up your game.

$

It was alleged in a recent biography that entrepreneur Elon Musk fired his assistant of 12 years after she asked for a raise. Elon allegedly told her to take 2 weeks off, during which he performed her duties himself. When she returned to work, Elon allegedly told her that he no longer needed her.

Elon Musk has denied this story as total nonsense. So let's give him the benefit of the doubt as he strives to save the human race from itself.

It's still a good example to get the point across about indispensability.

Try as hard as you can to be like Elon Musk.

$$\$$$

The important factor here is your attitude. Add value. Be helpful. Don't fight against your employers.

Here are some specific examples to give you the general idea.

$$\$$$

If you didn't finish everything you had to do at work today, stay a little longer. Take work home. Come in early.

Don't leave anything till the last minute. It will backfire.

$$\$$$

Make sure you achieve the end result. If your boss asks you to get a document from his lawyer, get the document from his lawyer. Don't just make a phone call. Don't just send an email. That's not what you were asked to do.

Keep following up until the end result has been achieved, ie. you have received the document and given it to your boss.

Companies reward results, not effort.

$

Stay focused. Don't let social media distract you. Distractions cause mistakes. You'll look bad. You'll feel worse. And you'll have to do it again, properly.

Don't spend hours on your phone, surfing the internet, or having long chats around the coffee machine. Don't dream about your weekend plans, or what you're having for lunch.

$

Don't get to work late then spend half an hour eating breakfast or getting dressed or putting on your makeup. Better yet, aim to be at work five minutes early, to cater for the occasional gremlin.

And don't sneak away early. That includes packing up early and watching the clock from a sprinter's crouch next to your desk.

$

Don't take all of your annual sick leave just because you can.

If you're on the road, don't sit in a café or bar, or go shopping or visiting friends all day.

Your employer doesn't pay you to do any of this, and it will be noticed.

$

Try to see things from management's perspective. Don't get twisted into the age-old conflict between management and workers. They have the money. You want some of it, or you wouldn't be there. You wouldn't be reading this book. Are you likely to receive more by digging in your heels and being a problem employee? Or by becoming a valuable team member and focusing on the job that puts money in your bank account and pays the bills?

$$\$$

Forget about your ego. This isn't about who's the better person.

Play the game. That's all it is. A game. With rules, and elements of luck. Opportunities and challenges. Learn the rules, look for the opportunities, and play to win.

$$\$$

If you want to get ahead, be promoted, earn a bigger bonus – focus on what you are supposed to be doing. If you can, expand your responsibilities to take on more important tasks within the organization.

Are you giving more than you're being paid? Probably. Is this fair?

Quick heads up – life isn't.

Will it pay off one day, in terms of recognition and financial rewards?

What's the alternative strategy? You could ask your boss to give you a raise or pay you overtime day after day because you didn't finish your work. Chances of success? Slim.

If none of these strategies work, don't change your attitude. Change your boss.

$

I'm not saying you should resign at the drop of a hat whenever things don't go your way. But if you're pouring your heart and soul into your work, day after day, doing everything right, and it's still not working, then eventually you will have to consider doing the same thing somewhere else.

$

Let's see... How else can I complicate your life?

If you get the chance – and you can make the time - study.

Remember not to take on too much. You might not use half of what you study. You may already know everything you need to know about your job. But that piece of paper can open doors and provide opportunities.

Full-time study will keep you from earning, and isn't for everyone. Consider studying part-time, while you're working. But first decide whether you can actually complete the course. Half a diploma is like being half-pregnant. It means nothing to anyone. The mere fact that you have the discipline to study while working will already impress potential employers.

But make sure your studies are meaningful and practical. There was a time when it seemed the only thing lawyers learned in college was how to ask if you wanted fries with that. Come to think of it, that's still the most useful phrase I've ever heard come out of a lawyer's mouth…

$

Ever wonder why actor Nicolas Cage works so hard?

He has earned more than $150 million during his career, and reputedly made $40 million in 2009 alone. But at one point he owed $14 million in back taxes, which he vowed to pay back in full. Hence his busy schedule.

Don't be like Nicolas Cage.

Chapter 9 – Decreasing Expenses

When it comes to building wealth, decreasing your expenses is as important as prioritizing savings and having the right attitude.

Think of it as retirement planning. All retirees want their overheads to be as low as possible. You won't have to keep earning more and more to pay the bills. You may even be able to retire early.

Decreased expenses = lower overheads = more financial freedom.

$

In this chapter, we are going to look at some common expenses that can usually be cut, resulting in extra savings.

Some cuts are small and (arguably, but really) easy to make. Morning coffee. Bank charges.

Others are big and hard, but potentially worthwhile. Selling the existing holiday home? A tough decision, but one that will pay off over the long term.

Some changes will be made as part of your new attitude. Skipping the annual cruise? Work out how much this money will have grown by the time you retire, and the decision becomes easier to make.

$

Do you love your Starbucks coffee in the morning? How much do you love it? Enough to give up your financial independence?

You do the math. The price of your daily cappuccino, times 4 (assuming you miss the odd day), times 40 (weeks), times 5 (years – conservatively). Or use 20 years instead of 5, to get an idea of how these small daily habits can add up over a lifetime.

That total should equate to a new small car. Paid cash.

And that's before we look at compounding. Over 20 years, let's be conservative and double that amount. Wow. Two cars. Or maybe even that Maserati you had your eye on.

Would it kill you to wait till you reached the office before you grabbed a cup? Or, if that's likely to result in a trail of dead bodies between your home and the office, make a cup at home and take it with you.

$

Try the same calculation with that McDonalds burger you grab every day for lunch. Compare it to the cost of a sandwich made at home, or (heaven forbid) a fresh salad.

Run the same calculation with any of your other regular habits. Smoking. Drinking. Chocolate bars. Newspapers. Magazines.

$

Does it hurt yet?

Welcome to financial responsibility 101.

Groucho Marx nailed it when he said that money will not make you happy, and happy will not make you money.

$

Who cleans your house? Who washes your clothes? Mows your lawn? Washes your car? Cleans your pool?

Don't hire home help just because the neighbours do. If you're really working so hard making money that you don't have the time to clean up after yourself – like, really – then carry on paying for help. As long as you keep in mind that the harder you work – in the office or at home – the more money you will save.

Run the same calculation as before. How much does it cost to have someone pick up your dirty socks 3 times a week? Over 20 years? Then double that amount.

Stop being a slob. Wash your own dishes.

If you have kids, teach them responsibility. Make it their problem. They won't break. Honest.

$

You don't need the latest iPhone as soon as it's released. I guarantee you. No matter who you are.

$

Clothing accounts? How many shoes do you need? Don't wear your clothes till they fall apart, but you don't need to shop for clothes every month. Close those accounts. Use your bank cards when you do need to shop.

$

Same goes for your other store accounts. Pay off the debt – even the interest free accounts - and use your bank cards. Take back control of your finances. You'll now know how much you have and how much you can spend.

$

Use those store loyalty points monthly. Don't wait till they build up to a huge number. It won't make you any wealthier, and they could expire.

$

Businesses exist to make money. This is the cornerstone of capitalism, which – for want of a better system – is what makes the world go round.

So banks will not lend you money for free. Your personal loan, your mortgage, your vehicle finance and your credit cards all cost you money in the form of interest.

Businesses who want to give you loans or open accounts for you are not doing it out of love. They are not your friends. You are too intelligent to fall for their tactics. So don't.

$

And don't fall for discounts. This includes Black Friday, emailed discount deals, and most store specials. If you were already planning to buy something, and you find it discounted, go ahead and buy it. An even better plan would be to deliberately wait until whatever it is goes on sale.

But if you were NOT already planning to buy something, the fact that it is on special means nothing to you. It will become an extra expense – costing you money – instead of saving you money by being discounted.

$$\$$$

Ignore marketing and advertising. These people are paid to take cash from your pocket. Those sparkling images and pretty colours are evil. Close your eyes. Cover your ears. Don't listen to the subliminal voices whispering at the back of your mind. You don't need everything they say you do.

$$\$$$

Watch your bank accounts. Make sure you are being charged the lowest bank charges possible for your needs.

$$\$$$

When initial contract periods expire, consider cancelling the debit order. Cellphone contracts, gym fees, magazine subscriptions, if debit orders are still running, make sure you are receiving value. Query any unusual transactions.

$$\$$$

Shop around for better rates on insurance, medical cover, gym fees. And do it again next year. And whenever your personal circumstances change. Marriage. Divorce. Childbirth.

HARD MONEY

But at the same time, make sure you have enough insurance & medical cover. This may often be a grudge purchase, but it could prevent a major financial setback.

$

Other setbacks could result from contractual obligations. Whenever you enter into this kind of agreement – an employment contract, rental lease, partnership agreement, marriage – make sure you have an appropriate exit strategy, agreed and documented up front.

Most people are too excited at the time to even think about this. They end up tied into restraints of trade, or lengthy notice periods. Or ex-wives who own everything they worked for. Be practical. Be smart. Be prepared.

$

Don't be like Marvin Gaye.

He declared bankruptcy in 1976 when he couldn't afford to pay back alimony amounting to $600 000. As part of the settlement process, he agreed that his ex-wife would receive the royalties from his next album, which included a song entitled "You can leave, but it's going to cost you."

According to Rolling Stone, Marvin lived in a bread van around this time...

$

Please note that, unlike marketing, credit cards are not evil. If they are used properly. Live within your means and settle the full balance as it becomes due every month.

Paying as much as you can by card – either credit card or debit card - also allows you to see where you spend your money. This will help you to draft an accurate budget (more on this later), which will be one of the cornerstones of your prioritized savings plan.

Credit cards also allow flexibility on the odd occasion when you do need to finance a large purchase, like car repairs. You can choose to pay this off over 2 or 3 months if you really have to, without applying for a loan.

Another advantage to using cards is that you may find yourself less inclined to indulge in impulse buying if you carry very little cash. It comes down to how much self-discipline you have.

$$\$$$

Look after your pennies and the pounds will look after themselves.

Keep your spare change in a jar, or the old traditional piggy bank. Bank it once you've filled the container. You'll be surprised how it adds up.

Check what you're charged at the till. Don't let the stores rip you off.

Buy books from a second hand store, or a local charity. If you can't be seen in either of those places, and would rather worry about what people might think - please refer to Chapter 1.

$

Finally, a word about tax.

Journalist P.J. O'Rourke tells us that giving money and power to government is like giving whiskey and car keys to teenage boys.

Yet give we must, if only to avoid being investigated later.

If the only two certainties in life are death and taxes, why don't we treat them the same? Nobody rushes into the reaper's arms at the first opportunity. We exercise. Eat healthy food. Schedule regular medical checkups.

Tax should be handled the same way. Accept that it's going to happen, but minimize the damage. Put it off as long as possible. Consult an expert.

$

Willie Nelson owed the IRS over $16 million in back taxes, penalties and interest. So in 1990, they raided his home and seized his assets. Willie managed to sing his way out of it, by selling some of his memorabilia and releasing an album called "The IRS Tapes," the proceeds of which were shared with the IRS.

Don't be like Willie Nelson.

$

You could wait till the new tax year to start building wealth.

Or when you receive your next bonus.

Or once you've paid off your car.

Or – you could start today. Right now. By actively doing something.

Like so many things in this book – and in life – this is entirely your choice.

Chapter 10 – Big Ones

Property and cars could be the most expensive items you ever buy. Excluding the jewellery, yachts, and private islands you may acquire one day after reading this book. So let's give them their own chapter and look at them in detail.

$

Always live within your means. Don't buy (or rent) a house where you can just barely afford the monthly payment. Interest rates WILL go up. You WILL have unforeseen expenses. Rates and taxes, and maintenance costs, WILL add to your total cost.

Same goes for your car. You don't need a Maserati. Until you can afford to buy it cash. And by then, you may no longer want it. You could be so locked into a pattern of living conservatively, being financially responsible, that you'll have to force yourself to live a little from time to time.

And you need to do that. Otherwise, what's the point of building wealth?

$

George Lorimer, editor of The Saturday Evening Post, reminds us that it's good to have money and the things that money can buy, but it's good, too, to check up once in a while and make sure that you haven't lost the things that money can't buy.

$

Should you own or should you rent?

Renting gives you more flexibility and mobility. But if you have settled on the area you'd like to live, and you plan to be there for a while, it usually makes more sense to buy. Instead of paying off someone else's mortgage, you'll be paying off your own.

$

If you do decide to buy a house, buy an inexpensive one in an expensive area. Let everyone else's properties increase the value of yours.

If you can, buy when interest rates are high. And/or when property prices are low. Don't buy the biggest house you can afford. Just because you qualify for a large mortgage, that doesn't mean you need to spend the full amount. Remember, banks are not your friends. Interest rates may fall eventually – along with your monthly mortgage payments – but they could go up first. Or later.

$

Settle your mortgage early, if you can. If your bank allows you to draw against these additional deposits, the cash will still be available if you need it for emergencies. Put your entire salary into your mortgage every month and save on interest until you need to take the money back to pay your bills.

But check with your bank first to ensure you have this kind of facility.

$

If you buy property in a secure complex, make sure the complex has a solid financial setup. High levels of cash in reserve mean you won't have to foot the bill when they need to fork out for urgent repairs.

$

Everything stated here applies to your primary residence, the house where you live. Buying property as a separate investment is a completely different ball game.

$

Nicolas Cage owned 15 residences, including a haunted mansion in New Orleans, an island in the Bahamas, and a castle in England. In 2006, he bought another castle, this time in Bavaria, and his luck turned. He sold the 28-room castle in 2009.

He declared bankruptcy the same year.

Don't be like Nicolas Cage.

$

There is money to be made in buying a property, renovating it, then selling it or renting it out. Using someone else's rental payments to settle your mortgage. Using the equity in your first property to finance another property.

But only if you know what you are doing. Property can also drain your cash when you need to dig deep to cover unexpected repairs, or when you have no tenant but still need to cover the mortgage. Property prices go down as well as up. So do interest rates.

$

Back in the 1970s, Arnold Schwarzenegger took advantage of the decade's high interest rates and invested heavily in property. Well done Arnold.

But twenty years later, along with Sylvester Stallone and Bruce Willis, he threw cash into the bottomless pit that was Planet Hollywood. The chain grew to contain 95 restaurants, then went bankrupt twice after drowning in huge debts.

Hasta la vista, baby.

$

Houses usually retain their value over time. Cars, not so much.

In fact, cars lose value as soon as you drive them off the showroom floor.

This is the asset category most likely to hold people back from their financial goals, purely because of the ego factor.

$

Consider buying a demo model. Or a good 2nd hand car. These will get you from A to B just as comfortably as that brand new Maserati. They will also take you further from $0 towards $1m.

$

HARD MONEY

Will the Maserati make you happy? Possibly. If you have your heart set on it, recognize that you are now choosing happiness over wealth. You have shifted your focus.

Nothing wrong with that. You will end up with less wealth at the end of the game, but this is your choice.

$

Financing a new car every few years is financial suicide. Pay one off. Then drive it. Not till it falls apart. Just till you've saved enough cash from the monthly repayments you used to make, to buy a new one for cash. Or at least put down a decent deposit.

$

Vehicle finance rates are generally lower than credit cards but higher than mortgages. It's a secured loan. The bank knows they can send a reality TV show around to take away your car if necessary. Unless you feel a burning desire to appear on reality TV, don't let that happen.

$

Take care of your car. Service it regularly. And trade it in on the next one. This makes it easier to pay cash.

And do you really need that high-octane fuel?

$

Nicolas Cage spent $450 0000 on the late Shah of Iran's Lamborghini Miura, to keep his 9 Rolls Royces company.

What happened to Nicolas Cage?

Do we want to be like him?

Chapter 11 – Budgeting

We've seen how small changes to your regular routine, extrapolated over time, can result in huge savings.

$

Income – expenses = surplus/ (shortfall). This is still a valid equation. Just not your main focus.

$

An occasional shortfall needs to be funded through debt or from your savings. A regular shortfall is a recipe for disaster, and a sign that you need to take action before it's too late.

But how will you know when this happens?

It's called a budget.

$

William Feather, the American publisher and author, says that a budget tells us what we can't afford, but it doesn't keep us from buying it.

Let's see if we can prove him wrong.

$

A budget is really just what you plan to do with your money for the foreseeable future. To get a starting point, you need to analyze your current spending patterns. Where does your money go every month?

Downloaded statements for credit cards and bank accounts can help you here. If you tend to spend mostly cash, try keeping the slips and analyzing them every month. Better yet, don't spend mostly cash.

$

When most of your spending is electronic, there are many online tools you can use to track it. Find one that works for you. Some of them will also help track your investments and debts, which we'll cover in the next chapter.

$

This part is important. If you don't know where your money goes, it will be that much harder to hold onto it.

$

The online tools are there. Many of them are free. All you need to do is choose to use them. Consistently. They may even suggest ways you can cut costs or earn more interest.

But remember – they are only tools. They can't force you to save. To focus. To adjust your attitude towards money. That remains firmly in your hands.

$

Whether you use an online tool, a spreadsheet, or pen and paper, you will now have a list showing your net income, what you take home after deductions, then your monthly expenses underneath.

Include all monthly payments – store accounts, loan repayments, and car payments. Use averages for expenses that fluctuate.

If your income is more than your monthly expenses, well done. You are on the right track. But you could still be doing better.

If your expenses are more than your monthly income, you know you have a problem. Maybe that's why you bought this book.

Okay, so let's see what we can do about it.

$

Whether your income is higher or your expenses are higher, you still need to run through those expenses on a regular basis and cut where you can. That's right, even if your income is already covering them.

Why? Because you could still be throwing money away every month.

Look critically at each expense. Is it essential? Phone around. Get comparative quotes. Are you buying expensive ready-prepared food when you could be cooking your own meals? Can you save on insurance? Is your car guzzling gas? Have the kids moved out, leaving you with a larger house than you need?

As mentioned previously, some of these are easier to change than others. But they all need to be questioned.

$

Cut where you can immediately. Put a plan in place to reduce the trickier expenses at an actual later date. Not "when you get around to it." Make a date with yourself now. Diarize it.

Have another look at the new budget. Are your expenses now less than they were? Less than your monthly income, if they weren't before?

If so, well done.

If not – keep going.

It is **essential** that you reduce your expenses. Initially, to an amount that's less than your income. At this point, you are breaking even. Then you need to keep widening the gap between income and expenses, till the expenses are as small as you can live with.

$

So far, this has been a theoretical exercise. Now we need to test it against reality.

Next month, compare your actual expenses against your budget. Did you manage to reduce and control your spending in the real world?

If so, well done.

If not – what went wrong? Was your budget unrealistic? You're sure? Being brutally honest with yourself? Okay, it's your budget. Adjust it. Then look at the new totals. Are your total expenses still less than your total income? Can you live with these numbers?

If so, well done. Carry on. Compare again in a month. And the month after that. And for as long as it takes for you to be confident that your spending is under control.

If not, we both know that you still have a problem. If, after all of these calculations, your total monthly expenses are still higher than your total income – you need to take drastic action.

$

Can you earn extra income? If you can find a part-time job (or a better permanent job) that increases your income above your expenses, that will solve your immediate problem. It might, for example, allow you to pay off old debts, putting you back on track to cover your normal monthly expenses.

But you still need to focus on those expenses.

$

Identify the problem. What can't be cut? If you are tied into contracts that you simply can't afford – possibly reckless lending on the part of your creditors - then it might be time to call for professional help. Consider debt counselling, where an expert will look at your finances and help you restructure where possible, in consultation with your creditors. This will cost you money and might not be as comfortable as doing it yourself using the pointers set out above. But it might be the only way to get you to the point where your income can cover your expenses.

$

As a last resort, you may have to consider declaring bankruptcy. This means that your debt will be wiped out, after you pay off as much as you can afford, and you get to start again. Except that you may have trouble buying on credit for a while, and any assets you had could be repossessed or sold to repay as much debt as possible. This is not the ideal solution, but sometimes it's the only solution. Try to avoid it, but don't panic if it happens. You'll be in good company.

$

Abraham Lincoln filed for bankruptcy twice. But under the laws of the time, he was taken to court and had to carry on repaying his debts for years.

Despite this, we could probably use a few more people like Abraham Lincoln.

Chapter 12 – How To Track It

Assets – liabilities = net wealth.

You need to know if you're moving in the right direction, or if you're going backwards. Maybe you're just treading water, and not moving in either direction.

You won't know unless you measure it.

Companies do this on a regular basis. One report shows how much profit or loss they made during a period. Another report shows their net asset position.

Their net wealth.

$

You can use one of the online tools discussed in the previous chapter. Or you can use a spreadsheet, or even an old-fashioned notebook and a pen.

List your house, car and jewellery at cost price. The car will decrease in value over time, but don't worry about that yet. Your big screen TV and sound system are not real assets for this exercise. Sorry.

Then list your bank accounts and investments (once you have some), showing current balances at the end of the month. Everything listed so far is an asset.

Under those amounts, list all your debt, showing current balances at the same date.

Total both groups of numbers. Subtract your total debt from your total assets. The net result is your net wealth.

$

Do the same exercise at the end of the next month. And every month after that, putting each month's numbers in a column to the right of the previous month's numbers.

If the net result is increasing, you are doing something right. You are on your way to building wealth.

If the net result decreases every month, you will have identified a problem that needs to be addressed. Go back to your budget. What went wrong? Was your income lower than expected? Or – more likely – did your expenses exceed your budget?

$

Ask yourself why it happened. Was it a once-off cost that affected one month in isolation? These things happen. Try not to have too many of them, but don't lose sleep over it.

Or was it a new monthly expense that you hadn't anticipated? Can it be reduced? If so, reduce it.

If not, update your budget. You might have to cut somewhere else to get yourself back on track. Hard choices. But necessary.

After implementing these changes, track the numbers again at the end of the next month. Were your adjustments successful in correcting the downward trend? Did your net wealth increase over the last month?

If so, carry on.

If not, repeat the steps listed above.

$

Enron was named "America's Most Innovative Company" by Fortune magazine for 6 consecutive years. Until 2001, when it came to light that Enron had been hiding several hundred million dollars' worth of losses and debts.

The company collapsed amid a barrage of legal cases and indictments.

Don't be like Enron's executives. Or their auditors. Be honest. Especially with yourself.

$

Now let's look forward instead of backwards.

Where would you like to be financially in 6 months' time? A year? 2 years?

Look at your monthly budget. Work out a sustainable monthly surplus. Increase it slightly, if you like a challenge. Then calculate how much you would like to have saved by your target date. Or how much debt you want to have settled by then. Or both.

Don't just plan to save whatever is left after paying the bills. That's not a plan. **Reprioritize your thinking.** Remember, saving is now your primary goal. Decreased expenses were just a means to an end, freeing up cash for you to increase your savings every month.

$

Early in your journey, you will have accumulated enough cash to pay next month's expenses in advance. Don't actually pay them in advance. Just have enough cash to be able to.

Congratulations. You are no longer living from paycheck to paycheck.

$

Reward yourself when you reach your milestones. Spend a little bit of that hard-earned cash. This should motivate you to carry on in the same direction. Bearing in mind that the more debt you settle, the more money you will have available to save. You will start earning more interest and paying less, and this effect will snowball over time.

$

Now push your savings till you have enough cash to pay 2 months in advance. Then 3 months. Then 6. Then 12.

This will double as an emergency fund when gremlins appear.

$

Your goals might seem small at first. Pointless. Your ultimate goals, unreachable. But you have to start somewhere. Baby steps.

Those hundreds you save over the first few months will turn into thousands soon enough. Then tens of thousands. Hundreds of thousands. Keep it up long enough and you may run into millions.

These are your first huge strides on the road to building wealth and becoming financially independent.

$

If you save less than you had planned to in any particular month, because of an additional expense that came out of nowhere – and these will happen – make it up over the next month or two. Don't lose sight of your savings targets. Get back on track as soon as possible.

$

Remember to take a break now and again. Reality check. Forget about the spreadsheet for a while. Breathe. Smell the roses.

Look around. Are your friends and family still there? Dog still recognizes you? Partner still smiling dreamily every morning?

So far, so good. Maybe you can keep some kind of balance after all.

Will everyone around you appreciate the hard work it took for you to reach this point? The stress, the sacrifices, the sleepless nights, the 12-hour days? Probably not. They'll think you're the luckiest person they know. They'll probably ask for some quick tips on how they can double their own money overnight.

Feel free to refer them to this book. Particularly Chapter 1.

Chapter 13 – What To Do With It Once You Have It

This book was written to help people manage their personal finances and their attitude to, and relationship with, money.

If you have followed the advice in the preceding chapters, and reached the point where you have a problem deciding how to diversify your growing investment portfolio, then my work here is done.

You will have broken your back to get here. You might look back and wonder whether it was all worth it. You certainly don't want to lose everything you've worked for through bad investment decisions.

$$\$$$

Sir Isaac Newton, one of the greatest scientific minds of all time, made huge profits from his investment in the 18th century South Sea Company. After withdrawing his money, he watched from the sidelines as the company's stock continued to rise in value. What to do in such a situation?

Sir Isaac jumped back in and bought more stock at more than three times what he had originally paid for it. When the bubble burst, he lost most of his life savings.

He allegedly stated, "I can calculate the movement of the stars, but not the madness of men."

Don't be like Sir Isaac Newton.

$

A proper financial plan, taking into account your unique circumstances and personal goals, is beyond the scope of this humble book. This was about saving, not investing. But investing is your next step.

Now you need to buy another book. From your local charity shop. (Sorry, old habits die hard)

Or you can find yourself a registered financial advisor. They can add value. They also charge fees. And they don't always get it right. Choose your advisor carefully, if you decide to go that route. Then listen carefully to what they have to say. If you're paying for their advice, use it.

$

When is it enough?

For some people, never. It can become addictive.

But in black and white mathematics, when you have enough capital to generate sufficient cash to cover your monthly expenses, then you should be in a position to sit back and enjoy the fruits of your labors.

You could generate cash from playing the stock market. Speculating on forex movement between currencies. Investing in small business ventures. Lending money to people.

Or you could set up a balanced, diversified investment portfolio and generate passive income and capital growth without lifting a finger. This might not bring in enough cash every single month, especially if you invest in stocks and bonds during turbulent times. You will have to work on averages over a period, keeping enough cash from the good months to cover the bad months. But it can be done.

$

The basics of investing are as simple as the basics involved in managing your day-to-day finances. Don't take too many risks. Stick with what you understand. If something seems too good to be true, it probably is.

$

John Malkovich, Steven Spielberg, Zsa Zsa Gabor, Kevin Bacon and many others lost millions in Bernie Madoff's $50 billion pyramid scheme. Madoff is currently serving a 150-year prison sentence.

Pyramid schemes – also known as Ponzi schemes – are not real investments. They have made many people rich, but have made more people poor. Those who get into the schemes early on tend to benefit. By the time the scheme collapses, those coming in at the end lose any money they put in.

Don't be like these silly rich people, who really should have known better.

Conclusion

Much of this book may seem to be nothing more than plain common sense.

That's because it is.

Stay focused. Work hard. Save your money.

We all know these rules. They are drummed into our heads, over and over again, from the time we start school.

But we forget the rules. We think we know better. We lose focus. And we wake up 40 years later wondering what happened to all the money we sold our dreams to make.

$

What else have we achieved along the way? Great memories? Old friends? Spiritual contentment?

None of these would be at all diminished if you had a little more money in the bank.

But those great memories and old friends didn't happen overnight. They took time. And hard work. Solid relationships are seldom easy.

$

Building wealth is the same. Anyone who wants to build wealth needs to focus on it as a conscious goal. Not an afterthought. Or they will muddle along through life and end up with whatever's left after spending most of it.

So focus. Define monthly and annual targets. Push those numbers. You will find a way to scrape together as much as you need to achieve your goals.

$

This book is not exhaustive. There are many ways to make more money and to cut costs. Babysitting. Walking dogs. Clipping coupons. Carpooling. Running weekly writers meetings. It would be impossible to cover them all.

And we haven't even touched on starting your own business, where you assume all the risk as compensation for potentially huge rewards. The principles we've discussed here apply to business owners as much as salaried employees.

$

The most important factor is your mindset. Your attitude. If you focus on building wealth as your number one priority, it **will** happen. If you lose focus, if you allow yourself to be distracted, it won't.

$

Even Warren Buffet, perhaps the most successful investor of our time, gets it wrong sometimes. His investment in Conoco Phillips lost him over $1 billion by 2012 when the oil price dropped and the company's stock fell accordingly.

HARD MONEY

Warren Buffet's number 1 rule was never to lose money.

His number 2 rule was never to forget rule number 1.

$

Of course, not everybody can be like Warren Buffet.

Some people will be better than others at building wealth. We can't all be champion bodybuilders. Or award winning musicians. But we can all be better at whatever we put our minds to. We can become the best we can be in any field, through years of dedication and practice.

Those who stay the course see the results. If you stop going to gym because your muscles hurt, you will never be Arnold Schwarzenegger. If you give up guitar lessons the first time your fingers blister, you will never be Jimi Hendrix.

$

Building wealth - delayed gratification - is just as hard. Hence the title of this book.

It might even be the hardest thing you ever do. There are few tangible benefits early on. Quite the opposite, in fact. Everyone around you will have better things than you. They will seem to live better lives. People can't help themselves. They judge what car you drive, where your kids go to school, where you live, what clothes you wear. Nobody sits around at dinner parties comparing bank balances or statements of net asset value.

$

Will Rogers, America's cowboy philosopher, said that too many people spend money they haven't earned, to buy things they don't want, to impress people they don't like.

$

If you save regularly, in a disciplined manner, prioritize your savings goals and control your monthly expenses, you have a good chance of building wealth over your working career. At the very least, you should be able to avoid the worst financial pitfalls that affect even the rich and famous.

Take control of your money. Make it work as hard as you did to earn it. Stop living from paycheck to paycheck.

With hard work, and a little luck, you **can** escape the rat race and live your dreams.

Last Word

But remember. It's just a game.

In the words of singer, novelist and politician Kinky Friedman - "Money can buy you a fine dog, but only love can make him wag his tail."

More From This Author

If you liked this book, you can find more of John West's work at

www.Amazon.com/author/Burning

www.Facebook.com/BurningRosesNovel

www.books449531774.Wordpress.com

$

Or scan the QR code on the next page for easy access to www.Linktr.ee/BurningRosesNovel - containing all the links above as well as links to Twitter, interviews, events, free giveaways and more.

$

Cheers.

HARD MONEY

www.ingramcontent.com/pod-product-compliance
Lightning Source LLC
Chambersburg PA
CBHW031540210526
45464CB00003B/1086